ALL THESE DAMN CATS

Written by
Doug Michael

Illustrated by
Amurtha Godage

I met a great girl, pretty as can be
We traveled all over, just her and me

It didn't take long though, to realize the fact
That soon I'd be dealing with all her damn cats

It started out slow, only just the one
I thought "this won't be that bad, maybe even fun"

Then more and more arrived, I was taken aback
Where'd they all come from all these damn cats

Now there are so many, I can't remember their names
When there's puke on the floor, which one should I blame

What's the skinny one called, why's this one so fat
I just can't keep track of all these damn cats

Could you stop at the store and get them some litter
Also food and a toy, one that looks like a critter

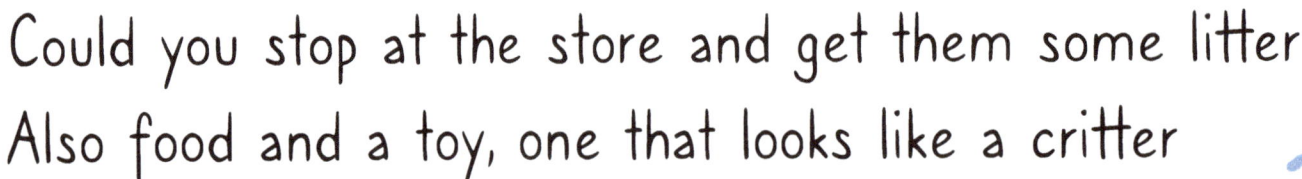

They need to pull their weight, catch some birds or a rat
What else are they good for, all these damn cats

My house plants chewed up, the others knocked on the floor
They try to act innocent as they sleep and they snore

We can't have anything nice, I say as a fact
As I clean up the mess of all the damn cats

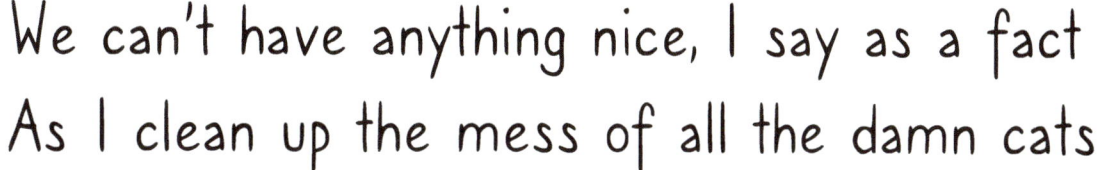

It's late in the evening trying to sleep in my bed
Slowly drifting off with happy dreams in my head

But I wake up with a gasp, one's on my face like a mat
They're trying to smother me, all these damn cats!

My alarms set for 5:00. Not a minute before
Until they scratch and they cry at a little past 4:00

I come back from the kitchen ones face deep in my drink
With a deep sigh I dump the whole thing down the sink

It's a little bit wasteful but they lick their own sacks
That's too much to share with all these damn cats

They stare while I poop, I just look at them and sneer
Would she even notice if maybe just one disappeared

I could leave the door open then do a surprised act
When she comes home to see there's no more damn cats

It must be great, this life that they're livin
Not a care in the world, not a crap to be given

Sleep and eat all day long, wish I could do that
I guess I'm just jealous of all these damn cats

I clean up their spills, their hair and their shit
I don't think they care, not one little bit

It's not that I hate them or want them to pass
They're just real annoying, all these damn cats

But when work's been rough, I come home angry and mad
Pour a tall whiskey and dwell on the day I've had

They curl up beside me I smile and give them a pat
I guess you're not so bad, all you damn cats

THE END